MW00888192

Lord

of the

Lawyers

By D.A. Morris

Copyright 2018

All rights reserved

Introduction: The "Christian Lawyer"

Christian + Lawyer

An oxymoron? Not the case. As the word order suggests, a Christian lawyer is first a Christian and second a practitioner of the law. In fact, a good attorney's training is a superb foundation for practicing not only law, but also faith. That's because attorneys have an appreciation of the concepts of authority, mercy, advocacy, and penalties. Together, they form "A MAP" toward understanding how Christianity can be a splendid guidepost in law practice.

Authority - *"I say to my servant, 'Do this,' and he does it"* (Matthew 8:9)

Mercy - *"the gift of God is eternal life in Christ Jesus our Lord"* (Romans 6:23)

Advocacy - *"if anybody does sin, we have an advocate with the Father—Jesus Christ, the Righteous One"* (Revelation 12:10)

Penalties - *"the wages of sin is death"* (Romans 6:23)

Nevertheless, if not properly used, a lawyer's skill comes with potential pitfalls. There's a legal impulse to poke and prod arguments to test their strength, and not always out of sincerity. Remember this dialogue in Luke 10, beginning in verse 25?

The Case of the Litigious Luke Lawyer

"On one occasion an expert in the law stood up to test Jesus. "Teacher," [the lawyer] asked, "what must I do to inherit eternal life?"

"What is written in the Law?" [Jesus] replied. "How do you read it?"

He answered, "'Love the Lord your God with all your heart and with all your soul and with all your strength and with all your mind'; and, 'Love your neighbor as yourself.'"

"You have answered correctly," Jesus replied. "Do this and you will live."

Given the Lord's answer, you might think that the case could be closed and the jury dismissed. Not so. This particular lawyer was litigious by nature, meaning, he was stoked for an argument. So he fired off a sneaky follow-up question.

But he wanted to justify himself, so he asked Jesus, "And who is my neighbor?"

Get that? The lawyer *"wanted to justify himself."* His objective really wasn't to find the key to eternal life, but to find a way to trip up Jesus. The lawyer's disingenuous question launched Jesus' teaching in what we refer to as the "Good Samaritan" parable. Jesus masterfully took the law expert to task, using an instructional method modern law schools call the "Socratic Method." Jesus described three different travelers who came upon a victim of highway robbery. Only one person stopped to help the victim. That helper was a member of the much-maligned, mixed-race, and mixed-faith people known as Samaritans. Of the three travelers, which included both a priest and a church official, the Samaritan was the least likely aid giver. But it was only the Samaritan who had mercy. Concluding His instruction, Jesus asked the lawyer a pivotal question in verse 36.

"Which of these three do you think was a neighbor to the man who fell into the hands of robbers?"

The expert in the law replied, "The one who had mercy on him."

Jesus told him, "Go and do likewise."

Case dismissed, at least for then.

Although the "lawyer" mentioned in this passage is not the courtroom litigator type we're familiar with, the Luke 10 lawyer was skilled at researching and applying Mosaic law. These essentially are equivalent to the skills modern lawyers deploy. A typical lawyer applies law to fact as she or he navigates through complicated legal systems. To help clients "win," the lawyer becomes an advocate. But the "Litigious Luke lawyer" exemplifies a unique vulnerability some lawyers have: a drive to self-justify rather than to submit to truth. Their well-honed skills as advocates may blind them to the fundamentals of Christianity, whose objective is not to flamboyantly "win" arguments or trip-up preachers, but to take the humble route toward serving God.

Is this just for lawyers?

No. This devotional is for anyone with a knack for cutting through to the root of an issue. It's geared toward anyone confronted with other peoples' demands from the moment they set their feet on the floor each day. That's why this devotional is brief. The format is simple. Each day has a verse of scripture, an application, and a closing prayer in plain talk. It's organized into seven sections of three meditations; one devotion per day for twenty-one days. Twenty-one, because it's said that it takes twenty-one continuous days of activity to develop a habit. With this in mind, this compact devotional provides a focused approach toward studying God's Word.

Have a reliable translation of the Bible handy. As with any faith guide, it's essential to be like the Bereans in Acts 17:11. Receive God's Word eagerly, but always examine the Scriptures to ensure that what your reference authority is saying is true. With something as crucial as eternal salvation at stake, everyone, not just lawyers, should be like the Bereans.

And that's a good habit to develop whether or not you're a lawyer.

Chapter One: Being Your Own Advocate

Before we can be the best we can be for family, church, clients, co-workers, and others, we have to be the best we can be for God. In turn, that makes us the best we can be for ourselves. This requires creating space for God to work within us. There are simple keys to doing this.

Getting away.

Praying.

Listening for direction.

The first part of this devotional is focused on who we are *vis-a-vis* God.

Day 1: Withdraw

Scripture:

"But Jesus often withdrew to lonely places and prayed...And the power of the Lord was with Jesus to heal the sick." Luke 5:16-17 (New International Version, "NIV")*

Application:

It may seem strange to begin program of building a stronger relationship with God by filing a motion to withdraw. But we can't be better at anything if our crowded calendar screams at us. No doubt, the pressures of living even the most normal of days drain us. Criticisms, burdens, work demands, costs of living, health challenges, social awkwardness, and so forth. It all adds up. Eventually, the mounting pressures threaten to break our ability to cope. But there's a Way not only to avoid breaking, but also to become charged-up stronger than ever:

Get away and pray.

Unplug, mute, run, walk—whatever it takes for you to have five minutes or so in prayer with God. Read through and meditate upon each day's devotional. If pressures seem too great to cope, call an immediate recess and have a private session with your Lord.

He's waiting.

Prayer:

I come to You, Dear Lord Jesus, just as You did, to find strength to be better today than yesterday. In Your Mighty Name I pray and believe, Amen.

*see Afterword

7

Day 2: What does God Want?

 **Scripture:**

"When the cool evening breezes were blowing, the man and his wife heard the LORD God walking about in the garden. So they hid from the LORD God among the trees." Genesis 3:8 (New Living Translation, "NLT")

"...for he knows how we are formed, he remembers that we are dust." Psalm 103:14 (NIV)

"My ears had heard of you
but now my eyes have seen you.
Therefore I despise myself
and repent in dust and ashes." Job 42:5,6 (NIV)

 **Application:**

What God wants from us has not changed since He created the first human:

He wants a relationship with us. (Genesis 3:8)

To be in a relationship with God, we first must acknowledge Who He is. He is the mightiest, most powerful Being in all existence. Yet, God also is the most loving Being of all. This loving God wants to be in an eternal relationship with us.

Now, what God *doesn't* want.

God doesn't want us to come to Him as if we've figured it all out. We needn't get all cleaned up with an attitude that we're in our "Sunday best" and presentable for Him. He's seen us at our worst. He knows that we're just dust. (Psalm 103:14)

And speaking of dust, some of us have to be brought back down to earth—literally in some cases. (Job 42:5, 6) Once we get that relationship right, and "come out of hiding" behind our false sense of self-importance, we're ready to engage in the best relationship imaginable, and it will last for eternity.

 **Prayer:**

Dear God, I haven't figured life all out. You know that. I come to You just as I am, praying that you will untangle me from earthly pressures and show me the light that leads to Your serenity. Amen.

Day 3: Convicted? But I'm a lawyer!

Scripture:

"And when [the Advocate] comes, he will convict the world of its sin, and of God's righteousness, and of the coming judgment." John 16:8 (NLT)

Application:

"Conviction" conjures up images of a courtroom gavel pounding and a strong criminal sentence being imposed. It signals wrongdoing. But that's not always a bad thing.

In fact, when we speak of being "convicted" by the Holy Spirit, that's a good thing. Somehow, somewhere, we've wandered and strayed into the dangerous territory of sin. But unlike a fallible criminal justice system, the Holy Spirit also gives us good, comforting counsel.

He encourages.

The Bible uses the Greek word *"parakletos"* in John chapters 14, 15, and 16 to describe the Holy Spirit. Translated, it means someone who is called to the side of another. The purpose is to provide counsel and support as well as issue an early warning of danger. That's why the Holy Spirit also is referred to as our "Advocate."

But we need positive feedback, too. God will provide us with encouraging feedback when we are pleasing to Him. (Matthew 3:17) Ask. (Matthew 7:11) How might He answer?

He probably won't speak in an audible voice thundering from the clouds. His answer may come from an unexpected encouraging word from a sister or brother in Christ (1 Thessalonians 5:11). Maybe, in our solitude, it will come from that warm, peaceful feeling we get while reading a passage of scripture (Philippians 4:17). Perhaps the melody or words of a song will stir our soul. Whatever form His positive feedback takes, it will come. That's the good thing about conviction, and God won't withhold any good thing from the righteous. (Psalm 84:11)

Go ahead. Ask for it.

 **Prayer:**

Father, I ask You to tell me not only when I'm doing wrong, but also when I'm doing right. Direct me as much as You can by positive reinforcement, but when I'm straying away, please have Your Holy Spirit correct me. Let Your conviction come as gently as possible, but as much as needed to get me back on track. Amen.

Chapter Two: Truth

Reading the headlines, it's easy to become disillusioned. Injustice and lies abound in this world. However, the beauty of Christianity is that it keeps us in the world, but not of the world. (John 17:14-15) That means we Christians are not detached from things going on around us. We're neither delusional nor in a perpetual state of denial.

But we don't let things going on *around* us *define* us.

Jesus prayed that we would be protected from the world's evil as we shined as inspired lights in the world's untruthful murkiness. (Matthew 5:16) This part of our devotional shows us where real truth lies, and the sometimes long journey through life that gets us there.

Another point about this section. Lawyers have specialized skills to make things better, not just for themselves, but for everyone valuing truth and justice. These values are especially relevant in the practice of law. The American Bar Association's Model Rules of Professional Conduct expressly emphasize the lawyer's special responsibility for *"the quality of justice."* Truth is core to justice, but as any experienced lawyer knows, justice is not guaranteed.

Day 4: Truth and Justice. Where?

 **Scripture:**

"Pilate said, 'What is truth?' Then he went back out to the Jews and told them, 'I find nothing wrong in this man. It's your custom that I pardon one prisoner at Passover. Do you want me to pardon the 'King of the Jews'?' They shouted back, 'Not this one, but Barabbas!' Barabbas was a Jewish freedom fighter." John 18:38-40 (The Message, "MSG")

"If they persecuted me, they will persecute you also..." John 15:20 (NIV)

"They tie up heavy, cumbersome loads and put them on other people's shoulders, but they themselves are not willing to lift a finger to move them." Matthew 23:4 (NIV)

"When one of you has a grievance against another, does he dare go to law before the unrighteous instead of the saints?" 1 Corinthians 6:1 (English Standard Version, "ESV")

 **Application:**

Over and over again, we see that there's no guarantee of justice from any government on earth, including the court system. Recall how Pilate convicted Jesus even though Pilate and his wife knew Jesus was innocent? (John 18:38-40) Jesus warned us that if they persecuted Him, the same would happen to us. (John 15:20)

We're not in heaven yet, so we can't expect heavenly justice. But don't despair. We can rely on one thing:

Everyone, including the corrupt, are under a higher authority.

At times, God allows the unfairness of the world to show us that our only hope is in Him. The evidence of injustice mounts and shows that we can't put our faith in mortal judges, juries, or leaders. As Christians, we should pray that God will intercede.

Understandably, these words may offer little comfort to

clients and acquaintances suffering from injustice. Accordingly, we must always strive to help those who are oppressed. That means using both prayer and our God-given skills to help others. Christians working tirelessly to help others may be the best representation of Christianity the world sees.

But, prayer is essential. If we truly believe in the mighty power of prayer, we must pray *at least* as much as we use our skills. Pray for our sisters and brothers in Christ. Pray also for rich and poor, black and white, western and non-western, southern nations and northern nations—everyone, including non-Christians. We must constantly pray that God will intercede for the rights of the downtrodden everywhere. When push comes to shove, we can't rely on the world to be fair to us or anyone we care about. (1 Corinthians 6:1-4)

**Prayer:**

Jesus, You told us we would experience persecution. Please direct me clearly on how to use my resources to set the oppressed free. Amen.

Day 5. No more loophole snooping

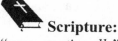 **Scripture:**

"*pray continually*" 1 Thessalonians 5:17 (NIV)

"*For precept must be upon precept, precept upon precept, line upon line, line upon line: here a little and there a little*" Isaiah 28:10 (King James Version, "KJV")

"*Study to shew thyself approved unto God, a workman that needeth not to be ashamed, rightly dividing the word of truth*" 2 Timothy 2:15 (KJV)

"*Therefore, there is now no condemnation for those who are in Christ Jesus, because through Christ Jesus the law of the Spirit who gives life has set you free from the law of sin and death*" Romans 8:1, 2 (NIV)

Application:

Learning about God and what's good for us takes a lifetime. Even mature Christians must learn to "walk according to the Spirit" and not the law. We're no longer looking for "technical compliance" with God's will, but spiritual unity with God. Sometimes, in order to serve God and others, we won't do something we want or have the right to do (legally, "forbearance"), even when there's no specific written passage of scripture that prohibits it. (1 Corinthians 8:9)

When God speaks, He will reveal the true purpose of His mission for each of us. He never will contradict His core purpose, but He will direct us in ways that a strict legalistic approach to religion might frown upon. In other words, He will show us how to correctly read, interpret, and follow His word.

Reaching this level of maturity takes time (Isaiah 28:10), regular bible study (2 Timothy 2:15), and continuous prayer (1 Thessalonians 5:17). As time passes, Jesus will reveal our unique missions.

 **Prayer:**

Father, I really want to understand and follow the real truth, which only comes from You. Lead me the right Way, and put me into contact with the right resources to know You. Give me the courage to follow through. Amen.

Day 6: Justified Anger at Injustice

 **Scripture:**

"God is a fair judge, a God who is angered by injustice every day." Psalms 7:11 (God's Word, "GW")

"For the Lord's sake, respect all human authority—whether the king as head of state, or the officials he has appointed. For the king has sent them to punish those who do wrong and to honor those who do right." 1 Peter 2:13, 14 (NLT)

"Pray this way for kings and all who are in authority so that we can live peaceful and quiet lives marked by godliness and dignity." 1 Timothy 2:2 (NIV)

"Jesus answered, 'You would have no power over me if it were not given to you from above. Therefore the one who handed me over to you is guilty of a greater sin.'" John 19:11 (NIV)

"I will punish the world for its evil and the wicked for their wrongdoing. I will put an end to arrogant people and humble the pride of tyrants." Isaiah 13:11 (GW)

"God wants you to silence the ignorance of foolish people by doing what is right." 1 Peter 2:15 (GW)

"And we know that in all things God works for the good of those who love him, who have been called according to his purpose." Romans 8:28 (NIV)

"Work hard to show the results of your salvation, obeying God with deep reverence and fear." Philippians 2:12 (NLT)

"But the LORD told Gideon, "There are still too many! Bring them down to the spring, and I will test them to determine who will go with you and who will not." Judges 7:4 (NIV)

 **Application:**

God puts governments in place. He sometimes allows bad governments, leaders, or adversaries to operate to fulfill His greater plan. (John 19:11; 1 Peter 2:13; 1 Kings 11:23; Jeremiah

27:6) They may be instruments used by God to do His work, whether they know it or not. Sometimes, that work may be "dirty work." Christians may not be well-suited to design and deploy the devices needed to counteract the forces of worldly evil.

That may be a hard thing to believe, but it's true and noted throughout the Bible. However, that doesn't mean that anyone should believe that all acts of all leaders at all times are justified merely because God allowed human free will to prevail. Especially *evil* free will. Use common sense. Since we don't always have the complete view of God's ultimate plan, we are to continue to fight for justice in accordance with His Word. (1 Peter 2:15)

Watch how God moves armies, legislators, and presidents around like chess pieces, strategically ensuring that His divine purpose becomes reality, right on schedule. (Romans 8:28) We don't see it in a snapshot. It develops like a serialized epic film.

As for the evildoers, they don't get off easy. Not one unjust action by the unjust goes unnoticed by God. In time, their every act will be judged in God's courts. The corrupt will meet His Supreme Justice. Sooner or later, they'll be punished for their evil deeds, even if God used their evil to bring about His good. (Isaiah 13:11: 14:5,6)

Meanwhile, we Christians must work hard for the oppressed to demonstrate the results of our being saved. (Matthew 5:16; Philippians 2:12) We also must pray for the victims, and pray that those in power will return to God's Way. (1 Timothy 2:2) We may be among the very few God selects to bring about His victory. (Judges 7:4)

 **Prayer:**

Dear God, I pray for victims of injustice. Empower me with tools, focus, and stamina to help them in my unique way. I pray for rule by good leaders, and that the bad ones will fall into Your plan quickly and not hurt the innocent. Amen.

Chapter Three: Testimony

In courtrooms, testimony is offered as evidence of a fact. Churches have "testimonies" in which the congregation offers statements of how God's goodness flourishes in their lives. Testimonies can encourage others, but if delivered the wrong way, to the wrong audience, or at the wrong time, they may not be effective.

As in a court of law, there's no "one-size-fits-all" formula on how to provide testimonial evidence. Let's explore how we can make ourselves living testimonies for the Lord.

Day 7: Your personal testimony comes in handy when---

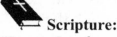 **Scripture:**

"I am a Jew, born in Tarsus of Cilicia, but brought up in this city. I studied under Gamaliel and was thoroughly trained in the law of our ancestors. I was just as zealous for God as any of you are today. I persecuted the followers of this Way to their death, arresting both men and women and throwing them into prison, as the high priest and all the Council can themselves testify. I even obtained letters from them to their associates in Damascus, and went there to bring these people as prisoners to Jerusalem to be punished." Acts 22:3-5 (NIV)

"About noon as I came near Damascus, suddenly a bright light from heaven flashed around me." Acts 22:6 (NIV)

"As Peter entered the house, Cornelius met him and fell at his feet in reverence. But Peter made him get up. 'Stand up,' he said, 'I am only a man myself.'" Acts 10:25, 26 (NIV)

"We too are only human, like you. We are bringing you good news" Acts 14:15 (NIV)

 **Application:**

All those "I's and me's" can be big turn offs if used the wrong way. Our past sometimes is the biggest stumbling block for people to believe us. We've lied, stolen, gossiped, cussed out, and failed, failed, and failed to keep our word so many times. But even those failures *may* help others, too.

When the message of Jesus is not accepted by those who hold onto their skepticism because of our past, we may not be the best messenger to deliver the Good News of the Gospel. But, if we are sure that God wants us to minister to a person, it may be the time to "address the elephant in the room."

Our history.

Only after prayer and leading by the Holy Spirit should we

put our past on display and declare, "that's the old woman/man, and that old person is dead." (Romans 6:6) That's what Paul was doing by describing his past evil acts in front of an angry mob in Acts 22.

Sometimes showing how far we've come will inspire others to do likewise. That journey should lead to the point where we had a change of heart, a change of mind, and a change of life. Like Paul's journey, that's our "road to Damascus" moment. (Acts 22:6) We may be surprised when our personal testimony breaks down walls that once kept our listener from accepting Christ's message of salvation. But that's a key distinction:

It's Christ's message, not ours.

We're humble servants. We must resist the temptation to put our lives front and center, whether it's our successes or failures. No matter how impressive our turn-around was, we're still fallible flesh. If we self-promote, others will pick and prod and find ways to topple us from our self-erected pedestals. That also gives detractors ammunition to turn away from the Gospel, as both Peter and Paul realized. (Acts 10:25, 26; Acts 14:15) All too often, the unsaved are looking for an excuse to resist Christ's personal calling to them. Don't give them more ammunition. Accordingly, a proper testimony is to show how Christ reached out even for us, and He is doing the same for everyone else.

**Prayer:**

Guide me, Jesus, on how to reach the people You want me to reach. Amen.

Day 8: Telling about Jesus, not ourselves

 **Scripture:**

"After the reading from the Law and the Prophets, the leaders of the synagogue sent word to them, saying, 'Brothers, if you have a word of exhortation for the people, please speak." ... *"Fellow children of Abraham and you God-fearing Gentiles, it is to us that this message of salvation has been sent."* Acts 13:15, 26 (NIV)

 **Application:**

As we've studied yesterday, there are times when it's helpful to share our personal testimony regarding our own sinful lifestyle before being saved. But that's not always the case. Sometimes we have to give our own story the backseat, or no seat at all. There's a great example in scripture.

Even though Apostle Paul often told how he was an enemy of Christ and persecutor of the budding church, he sometimes told the history of God's plan of salvation without mentioning his own conversion story to his audience. And his story, of course, is breathtaking. But it wasn't always in the best interest to share it. We should apply Paul's examples in our own ministry.

- We tailor the story of God's wide offer of salvation to the people He wants us to reach.
- We don't draw unnecessary attention to ourselves.
- We let God's story take center stage so that people can apply it to their own lives.

Through this, we minimize the likelihood of distracting or discouraging some people. If needed, there will be plenty of time to counsel others with our personal stories. But until we receive confirmation from the Holy Spirit, it's best to let the Bible speak for itself.

**Prayer:**

Inspire me to speak Your Word the right Way, at the right time, and to the right audience, all according to Your will, dear Lord and Savior Jesus Christ. Amen.

Day 9: The testimony of inadequacy

 **Scripture:**

"But he said to me, "My grace is sufficient for you, for my power is made perfect in weakness." Therefore I will boast all the more gladly about my weaknesses, so that Christ's power may rest on me." 2 Corinthians 12:9 (NIV)

"Do you see a person wise in their own eyes? There is more hope for a fool than for them." Proverbs 26:12 (NIV)

 **Application:**

How do we testify when we feel inadequate?

First, realize that testimonies are not always success stories, at least not at face value. Some of the best testimonies are based on failures. Sharing our feelings of inadequacy may help others. Everyone can relate. If we want to become better in some targeted area, we have to be around people whom we perceive as better in those areas than ourselves. That means we will feel inadequate.

Consider Paul, again. As far as credentials are concerned, Paul was among the most learned of all Jews, *"although I myself might have confidence even in the flesh. If anyone else has a mind to put confidence in the flesh, I far more."* (Philippians 3:4). Paul's pedigree was impeccable, but even he believed his worldly accomplishments were no better than filthy rags. (Isaiah 64:6; Philippians 3:7) Why?

Paul felt humbled by the mission Christ gave him, *"Unto me, who am less than the least of all saints, is this grace given, that I should preach among the Gentiles the unsearchable riches of Christ"* (Ephesians 3:8)

Paul didn't see himself as the world saw him, but as he thought he *should be*, given his mission. No matter how much he accomplished, he would not feel "worthy."

That's good.

Humility drives us to Christ, Whose sacrifice and power are all that matter. We get better by allowing humility to propel us to Christ's higher power. Feeling inadequate may generate the most effective testimony of all. Further, feeling inadequate may even motivate us to become more effective in the pursuits we want to do most.

 **Prayer:**

Father, help me understand that the feelings of inadequacy that I have are not always bad. Through my humility, I grow in my ability. I give You all the glory. Amen.

Chapter Four: Service

Service to others is key to a lawyer's professional responsibilities. But serving should be key to anyone's life, both personal and professional. After all, what good is life if it's lived only for selfish indulgences? The result is emptiness, loneliness, mistrust, alienation, and anguish. Reading the Book of Ecclesiastes is proof.

"...when I surveyed all that my hands had done and what I had toiled to achieve, everything was meaningless, a chasing after the wind; nothing was gained under the sun." Ecclesiastes 2:11 (NIV)

But whom should we serve? The Luke 10 "Good Samaritan" parable mentioned in the introduction is a superb eye opener, and *heart* opener, as well. When we get the right attitude about what "serving" really means, the answer may surprise us.

Day 10. Service, not slavery. Discipline, not punishment

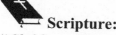 **Scripture:**

"Children, obey your parents in everything, for this pleases the Lord. Fathers, do not embitter your children, or they will become discouraged." Colossians 3:20-21 (NIV)

"Therefore we do not lose heart. Though outwardly we are wasting away, yet inwardly we are being renewed day by day." 2 Corinthians 4:16 (NIV)

 **Application:**

Childhood is the perfect time to understand the nature of our relationship with God:

- We are not set on being slaves, but *servants* learning to put others' interests above our own.
- God is not set on punishment, but *disciplining* to shape us into better people.

The distinctions are very real. Here's good news: we're always children to God (1 John 3:1). That means we are always in the mission of serving and discipline. Although the world may get worse, and even our bodies may age, our spirits become stronger. This attitude helps us as we strive to help others.

 **Prayer:**

Dear Father in Heaven, when I go astray, please clearly but gently discipline me to get back onto the righteous path. Help me as I use my talents and gifts to serve others. Amen.

Day 11: Serving our way toward appreciation

 **Scripture:**

"Jesus called them together and said, 'You know that those who are regarded as rulers of the Gentiles lord it over them, and their high officials exercise authority over them. Not so with you. Instead, whoever wants to become great among you must be your servant, and whoever wants to be first must be slave of all. For even the Son of Man did not come to be served, but to serve, and to give his life as a ransom for many.'" Mark 10:41-45 (NIV)

"Open your mouth for the mute, for the rights of all who are destitute. Open your mouth, judge righteously, defend the rights of the poor and needy." Proverbs 31:8-9 (ESV)

"Be careful not to practice your righteousness in front of others to be seen by them. If you do, you will have no reward from your Father in heaven. So when you give to the needy, do not announce it with trumpets, as the hypocrites do in the synagogues and on the streets, to be honored by others. Truly I tell you, they have received their reward in full. But when you give to the needy, do not let your left hand know what your right hand is doing, so that your giving may be in secret. Then your Father, who sees what is done in secret, will reward you." Matthew 6:1-4 (NIV)

"In everything I did, I showed you that by this kind of hard work we must help the weak, remembering the words the Lord Jesus himself said: 'It is more blessed to give than to receive.'" Acts 20:35 (NIV)

Application:

Everyone wants to be appreciated. But there's a distinction between appreciation and exaltation. How do we distinguish a healthy desire for appreciation from a dangerous need to be singled out and put on a pedestal in front of others?

Jesus is our model.

He said that if someone wants to be great, he must serve others. Lawyers and other professionals hold secular keys to help free the oppressed from the world's tricky rules and traps. Freed, many of these people realize how God uses professionals to help them. They, in turn, are inspired to help others. As an added bonus to the helpers, humble service opens the floodgates of appreciation that the human spirit craves.

That's another reason why it's better to give than to receive. (Acts 20:35)

**Prayer:**

Dear Lord, I'm grateful for the gifts and talents You've given me. Please remind me daily that without You, I'm helpless, and with You, I can help so many more people than just myself. Amen.

Day 12: The hymn of Godly deeds

 **Scripture:**

"Learn to do right; seek justice. Defend the oppressed. Take up the cause of the fatherless; plead the case of the widow." Isaiah 1:17 (NIV)

"Keep on loving one another as brothers and sisters. Do not forget to show hospitality to strangers, for by so doing some people have shown hospitality to angels without knowing it. Continue to remember those in prison as if you were together with them in prison, and those who are mistreated as if you yourselves were suffering." Hebrews 13:1-3 (NIV)

 **Application:**

Although God loves our Sunday morning choruses of "Amazing Grace," He takes at least as much joy when we awaken each morning, give Him praise, and ask Him for guidance as we serve others with Godly deeds done in humble, God-steered ways. Serving others includes serving the prisoners, broken families, strangers, poor, sick, and lonely. God's love spans across neighborhoods, ethnicities, ages, incomes, and even religious beliefs. Let our love follow His love as we live out our personal hymns through service.

Prayer:

Please, dear Father, inspire me today to live out my own hymn of Godly deeds. Amen.

Chapter Five: Identity

There's a Latin phrase in law, *res ipsa loquitur,* which translates "the thing speaks for itself." It's used primarily to presume negligence when the face value of something tells a story all by itself.

We have face value, too.

We can choose to show the world the face of misery, happiness, or anything else merely by our disposition, words, or actions.

That's our identity.

Everyone should take time to identify their special gift or talent that's useful to help others. When we serve, we are in a sense "ambassadors" identified by our Christianity. Yet our Christianity doesn't call for us to compromise our unique personalities. In fact, our personalities may be exactly the tools God uses to reach out to people unreachable by others. Face value can open the doors to blessings.

Day 13: God, free will, and our own personalities

 **Scripture:**

"For as in one body we have many members, and the members do not all have the same function, so we, though many, are one body in Christ, and individually members one of another. Having gifts that differ according to the grace given to us, let us use them..." Romans 12:4-6 (ESV)

 **Application:**

God doesn't force us to do anything, including to serve Him or to love Him. God knows our personalities with 100% accuracy. He knows how we'll react in any given situation.

That's how He uses us. He allows our natural personalities and inclinations to operate, whether for good or bad.

God uses our free will to advance His divine purpose. If we confess Jesus as our Lord and Savior while voluntarily submitting to His divine will, He will take us into His hands and gently shape us into His image. As a result, we're useful for good works...with our unique personalities shining bright.

 **Prayer:**

Loving Father, I'm glad You love me so much that You don't make me conform. On my own free will, I choose to be molded by You so that I can serve You and do something every day to make the world a better place in accordance with Your will. Amen.

Day 14: No one is a foreigner to God

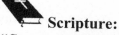 **Scripture:**

"So we are Christ's ambassadors; God is making his appeal through us. We speak for Christ when we plead, "Come back to God!" 2 Corinthians 5:20 (NLT)

"He defends the cause of the fatherless and the widow, and loves the foreigner residing among you, giving them food and clothing. And you are to love those who are foreigners, for you yourselves were foreigners in Egypt." Deuteronomy 10:18-19 (NIV)

"When a foreigner resides among you in your land, do not mistreat them. The foreigner residing among you must be treated as your native-born. Love them as yourself, for you were foreigners in Egypt. I am the Lord your God." Leviticus 19:33-34 (NIV)

 **Application:**

The 1961 Vienna Convention on Diplomatic Relations put into writing the ancient custom of providing a place of refuge for people in a hostile foreign land. These places of refuge are known as embassies, and ambassadors direct them. No matter how hostile the outside environment may be, even local police and military in the embassy's host nation aren't permitted to enter and seize the refugee.

We once were refugees, but God had mercy on us. He took us into His safe haven. We are saved, and now we are ambassadors of Christ.

Every day we discover people under siege. One child tiptoes around undetonated mines in South Sudan as another drifts toward the rocky shores of Greece. A grandmother cowers in the darkness of a south Texas truck trailer while a young man swelters in a North Korean prison. Maybe someone in our own neighborhood flounders in dire straits.

Different physiological features, different places of origin, and different cultures. Some are Christians, some are not. They all need the Lord's protection. They could use our help and direction to get there.

God doesn't force us to react to them in any particular way. But He clearly shows us His Way. Are we living our lives so that the world sees our ambassadorship?

**Prayer:**

Dear Father, I pray that I'll be more like You to those who are not like me. Amen.

Day 15: Knowing and known by Jesus

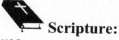 **Scripture:**

"Not everyone who says to me, 'Lord, Lord,' will enter the kingdom of heaven, but only the one who does the will of my Father who is in heaven. Many will say to me on that day, 'Lord, Lord, did we not prophesy in your name and in your name drive out demons and in your name perform many miracles?' Then I will tell them plainly, 'I never knew you. Away from me, you evildoers!' Matthew 7:21-23 (NIV)

 **Application:**

At funerals, so many references are made about Jesus Christ and the person who has passed away. But what about that period between birth and death? How often did that person refer to Jesus Christ? Did Jesus know the sound of that person's voice as she or he prayed to Him for direction? How often did the person give thanks to the Lord?

No matter how impressive our resumes are, we're shallow failures unless we've lived in a relationship with the Lord. Live it.

It's better late than never, of course, but it's much better early than late.

Prayer:

Jesus, I know Your Name. Please encourage me to call upon it daily. Hear my prayers that this evil-soaked world will repent, know You, and be known by You. Amen.

Chapter Six: Red Herrings of the World

Law teaches that red herrings are statements meant to throw an investigator off the trail. Red herrings themselves may be non-lethal, but at the end of the trail, there's hell to pay.

The best remedy for a red herring is to take the true path and stay on it. That true path is not found by following what the world says, but what God's Word says.

Day 16: Doing what's right in our own eyes (and ears)

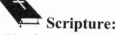 **Scripture:**

"In those days there was no king in Israel. Everyone did what was right in his own eyes." Judges 17:6 (ESV)

"For the time will come when people will not put up with sound doctrine. Instead, to suit their own desires, they will gather around them a great number of teachers to say what their itching ears want to hear." 2 Timothy 4:3 (NIV)

Application:

No matter the era, people have sought spiritual leaders who would tell them what they wanted to hear. In the Old Testament, priests were bought under the guise of having them deliver the God's prophecy. In reality, they were expected to prophecy what the hearer wanted to hear. (Judges 17:10-13; 1 Kings 22:8)

These days, with instant access to our preacher-of-choice, it's easier. We can log in 24/7 to a spiritual guru who'll make us feel great about ourselves. That's a fake faith fix. This condition, known as "itching ears," is as old as the church. (2 Timothy 4:3) We get false comfort when the preacher quotes scripture out of context or uses flowery, Shakespearean language that sounds like scripture, but isn't. Scratching those itching ears by not studying the Bible ourselves comes with dire consequences.

Reading just parts and not the whole of scripture skews the Word. Twisting the Bible may back up practically any wicked behavior. Furthermore, we miss out on the absolutely beautiful unity of God's Word and His comforting instruction to us for all times.

Like the Bereans mentioned in the introduction, we must avoid scriptural illiteracy and search the Bible ourselves. (Acts 17:11) Most of all, we must pray that we'll follow God's directions when He leads us to the only truth that exists: Himself.

**Prayer:**
Dear Lord, I pray that I'll not seek what I want to hear, but what You want me to hear. Amen.

Day 17: Paganism in our developed country lives

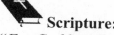 **Scripture:**

"For God knows that when you eat from [the tree of knowledge] your eyes will be opened, and you will be like God, knowing good and evil." Genesis 3:5 (NIV)

"Therefore, my dear friends, flee from idolatry...you cannot drink the cup of the Lord and the cup of demons too; you cannot have a part in both the Lord's table and the table of demons. Are we trying to arouse the Lord's jealousy? Are we stronger than he?" 1 Corinthians 10:14, 21,22 (NIV)

"How art thou fallen from heaven, O Lucifer, son of the morning! how art thou cut down to the ground, which didst weaken the nations! For thou hast said in thine heart, I will ascend into heaven, I will exalt my throne above the stars of God: I will sit also upon the mount of the congregation, in the sides of the north: I will ascend above the heights of the clouds; I will be like the most High." Isaiah 14:12-14 (KJV)

"As it is written: 'There is no one righteous, not even one.'" Romans 3:10 (NIV)

 **Application:**

We make the mistake of thinking that pagan idols are crudely carved wooden images found in remote villages populated with "naked savages." But the most dangerous pagan idols aren't the carved wooden figurines dedicated to Baal, an animal, or some other figure. In fact, the most dangerous idols aren't physical objects at all.

Anything that demotes God from His supreme authority and promotes us as little gods is a pagan idol. Modern-day pagan idols of developed country cultures include:

- self-promotion (Isaiah 14:12-14);
- the power of our self-driven actions, words, positive thinking, or the "indomitable human spirit" (Ephesians 2:8);
- wealth and accumulation of "stuff" as our little kingdoms (Matthew 6:24);
- the belief that any human, world government, or political system is itself worshipfully divine (Acts 12:21-23); and
- the belief that people, by nature, are good and can deliver the world to paradise. (Romans 3:10)

These all overlap. There is one core trait that is shared by them all, and it is at root of the original sin in Genesis 3:5:

They exalt human ideologies, powers, and ultimately, ourselves, over God.

Looked at this way, those crudely carved wooden images are easier to destroy than these developed country pagan idols.

 **Prayer:**

Dear Lord our God, please help me recognize, and give me the power to destroy, the pagan idols that are in and around my life. In Jesus' name, Amen.

Day 18: I'm OK, but you're not

 **Scripture:**

"To some who were confident of their own righteousness and looked down on everyone else, Jesus told this parable: "Two men went up to the temple to pray, one a Pharisee and the other a tax collector. The Pharisee stood by himself and prayed: 'God, I thank you that I am not like other people—robbers, evildoers, adulterers—or even like this tax collector. I fast twice a week and give a tenth of all I get.' "But the tax collector stood at a distance. He would not even look up to heaven, but beat his breast and said, 'God, have mercy on me, a sinner.' "I tell you that this man, rather than the other, went home justified before God. For all those who exalt themselves will be humbled, and those who humble themselves will be exalted." Luke 18:9-14 (NIV)

 **Application:**

There's nothing easier to do than find a terrible example of human failings and claim that we are better. Smugness is dangerous. It leads us to believe that God's work on us is finished and we can rest while picking out the faults of others. A better perspective begins with realizing how, despite our own failures, God still loves us. True love toward God will make us want to do better. Humbling ourselves is far better than being humbled by God. (Matthew 21:44)

 **Prayer:**

Father, I pray that I will never dwell on others' shortcomings more I dwell on my own. Thank You for having mercy on me. Amen.

Chapter Seven: Closing Argument and Verdict

By now, it's obvious that this devotional is not designed to convince readers that God exists. There are numerous fine books that go into those points. Here, as a devotional, our objective is to add focus and development in our walks with Christ. This is particularly important for lawyers and other professionals. But professionals live most of their days providing "objective evidence" to serve clients. After all, we're still "in" the world, and so are our clients and acquaintances counting on us. (John 17: 15, 16)

This last section addresses the need for balance.

Day 19: Proof

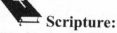 **Scripture:**

"Indeed, when Gentiles, who do not have the law, do by nature things required by the law, they are a law for themselves, even though they do not have the law. They show that the requirements of the law are written on their hearts, their consciences also bearing witness, and their thoughts sometimes accusing them and at other times even defending them." Romans 2:14,15 (NIV)

"Jesus answered, 'I am the way and the truth and the life. No one comes to the Father except through me.'" John 14:6 (NIV)

"For what can be known about God is plain to them, because God has shown it to them. For his invisible attributes, namely, his eternal power and divine nature, have been clearly perceived, ever since the creation of the world, in the things that have been made. So they are without excuse." Romans 1:19, 20 (NIV)

"Here I am! I stand at the door and knock. If anyone hears my voice and opens the door, I will come in and eat with that person, and they with me." Revelation 3:20 (NIV)

Application:

Look around. We're social beings. Things go horribly wrong when one of us drops out of healthy social relationships. Our consciences are troubled. Our compassion for fellow humans crumbles. We self-destruct. But those are dire symptoms of a deeper, more sinister issue: Being out of relationship with God.

There lies the root cause of all moral decay, social imbalance, and self-hatred. There's a remedy available to anyone:

Go back to God.

God created the Way back to Him the moment we committed the first sin. Jesus Christ is the Only Way back into fellowship with God. Want proof? Look around.

**Prayer:**

Father God, I am surrounded by every indication of Your existence. I see, know, and feel Your creation and Your love. I also see the misery that comes from not being in fellowship with You. Through Jesus, I pray to be always in a healthy relationship with You, and I offer myself as a route to show others the Way to Jesus. Amen.

Day 20: The verdict

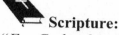 **Scripture:**

"For God so loved the world that he gave his one and only Son, that whoever believes in him shall not perish but have eternal life. For God did not send his Son into the world to condemn the world, but to save the world through him. Whoever believes in him is not condemned, but whoever does not believe stands condemned already because they have not believed in the name of God's one and only Son. **This is the verdict:** *Light has come into the world, but people loved darkness instead of light because their deeds were evil. Everyone who does evil hates the light, and will not come into the light for fear that their deeds will be exposed. But whoever lives by the truth comes into the light, so that it may be seen plainly that what they have done has been done in the sight of God."* John 3:16-21 (NIV)

"Then he told me, "Do not seal up the words of the prophecy of this scroll, because the time is near. Let the one who does wrong continue to do wrong; let the vile person continue to be vile; let the one who does right continue to do right; and let the holy person continue to be holy." Revelation 22:10-11 (NIV)

Application:

Christianity gives no surprises as to what will happen after we pass from this life. We know the judgment upon us by the way we live on earth. Have we confessed that Jesus is God's Son, our Savior Who rose from the dead, and is the Source of our eternal salvation? Do we really believe this? If so, we will live with Him eternally in His kingdom. We don't rely on our deeds to get us there. Nor do we rely on the prayers of those left behind us on earth.

We enter the light of God's kingdom because we accept that Jesus is the only Way, He is truth, and He is life. (John 14:6)

Let's not be fooled by those who say it takes more. (Romans 10:9)

Although we have human failings, we live our lives hating evil. God's plan provides a plain and accessible Way for anyone who wants to have it. It's not "sealed up" in secrecy. Believers know that they have been saved and will live in God's kingdom forever.

The unfortunate flip side is that vile wrongdoers are free to continue to do things that God hates. They know the consequences. Their fate is not hidden, either.

The verdict? One Way or the other, there's no surprises.

 **Prayer:**

I thank You, Father, for the eternal gift of life with You. I pray that many others will accept You also. Amen.

Day 21: Many Ways to Jesus, but One Way to God

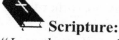 **Scripture:**

"I am the way and the truth and the life. No one comes to the Father except through me." John 14:6 (KJV)

 **Application:**

E pluribus unum

Most of us see this phrase nearly every day. It's on the Great Seal of the United States. It appears on money, podiums, medals, carpets, and government documents. The Latin phrase means, *"out of many, one."* Although its origin stretches back to before the original thirteen colonies of the United States, it can serve as a reminder of a much, much more profound truth:

There are many Ways to Jesus, but there's only One Way to God.

Jesus Christ.

Look at scripture. A blind beggar met Jesus on the road. A paralytic came in to Him through the roof. A Samaritan woman found Him at a well. Matthew the tax collector met him at his collection booth. An adulterous woman fell at His feet as her accusers dragged her through the dust. Paul the Apostle witnessed Him on the Road to Damascus. Pilate confronted Him on the imperial court. Two thieves hanged with Him on the Cross.

Not everyone accepted Jesus as Savior, but all encountered Him in a unique Way.

The same applies now. We need not see Jesus physically to be in His presence, but everyone on earth has an opportunity to meet Him. (e.g., Romans 2:15) Some meet Him in their deepest moments of depression. Others during a relaxing vacation. Some surf television channels, radio stations, web pages, or podcasts and discover Who Jesus is. Maybe a family member, friend, or acquaintance will offer a book or scriptural passage to ponder.

There are many, many Ways to get to Jesus. Or, more accurately, there are many Ways that Jesus politely *makes His presence known to us.* (Revelation 3:10)

But there is no Way to be in contact with God other than Jesus.

There are many religions, belief systems, and philosophies, but only in Christianity does God Himself, the Creator of everything, come down to earth and become human in order to save the entire world…and introduce Himself to us in the flesh.

Why?

Because He desires the exact same thing He wanted when He created the first human. He wants a loving One-on-one relationship with everyone in existence, now or ever. Only Jesus is the Way, the truth, and the life.

Out of many,
One,
and out of One,
God

 **Prayer:**

Father, thank You for giving me the opportunity to meet Jesus and accept His offer of salvation. I confess and believe that Jesus Christ, Your Son, came in the flesh, died for my sins, and You raised Him from the dead. Now, I gladly offer You myself, washed clean by the blood of Your Son and my Savior, Jesus Christ. Amen.

Afterword

Thank you so much for taking this journey with me. I pray that something in this devotional has inspired you to study the Word of God for yourself and continue on your unique journey of service to Him and others.

D.A. Morris

2018

Notes:

"Way" is capitalized often here, drawing upon Christianity's early history, when Christians were referred to as followers of *"The Way."* This pertains to Jesus Christ's declaration *"I am the way, the truth, and the life."* (John 14:6 NIV*) "He" "You"* and other pronouns similarly are capitalized when referring to the Divine.

Bible Translations used in this devotional:
- NIV - New International Version
- KJV - King James Version
- ESV - English Standard Version
- GW - God's Word
- NLT - New Living Translation

Justice and service as part of lawyers' model practice:

The Preamble of The American Bar Association's Model Rules of Professional Conduct states *"(1) a lawyer, as a member of the legal profession, is a representative of clients, an officer of the legal system and a public citizen having special responsibility for the quality of justice...(6) As a public citizen, a lawyer should seek improvement of the law, access to the legal system, the administration of justice and the quality of service rendered by the legal profession."* The ABA House of Delegates adopted the rules in 1983. They serve as models for the ethics rules of most jurisdictions.

D.A. Morris is a Christian attorney, church elder, writer, and world traveler.

damwriter.com